OK, BUT WHAT DOES A JUDE DO?
Copyright © 2023 by ROGER H. PONCE JR.

All rights reserved. No part of this book may be reproduced or transmitted in any form or by any means without written permission from the author.

ISBN: 9798376424230
Imprint: Independently published

A judge dons a black robe to do what they do.

A judge has a courtroom they command with might.

They sit on a *dais*. The plathform raised ...

A judge converses with marshals, bailiffs, and clerks...

When two sides dispute and can't find a way...

A judge can step in to resolve and to sway.

If mischief you've made and trouble ensues...

A judge shall decide which time-out to choose.

Decisions can be hard and may feel unfair...

But they have to be made and a judge can help there.

Interpreting law today for tomorrow and generations too.

Laws affect all aspects of life. In school, home, out and about, the law affects your rights.

Laws and constiutions shall be applied, without fear or favor, a judge must decide.

So it is important to know just what they do...

www.ingramcontent.com/pod-product-compliance
Lightning Source LLC
Chambersburg PA
CBHW051836210526
45473CB00005B/1902